AMAZING ANIMALS

ORANGUTANS

BY MARI BOLTE

CREATIVE EDUCATION • CREATIVE PAPERBACKS

Published by Creative Education
and Creative Paperbacks
P.O. Box 227, Mankato, Minnesota 56002
Creative Education and Creative Paperbacks
are imprints of The Creative Company
www.thecreativecompany.us

Design by The Design Lab
Production by Blue Design
Art direction by Wyeth Morgan

Images by flickr/Biodiveristy Heritage Library, 8; Getty Images/AlonzoDesign, 2, 3, 4, 6, 7, 8, 10, 11, 12, 13, 14, 15, 16, 18, 19, 20, 22, 24, Cavan Images, 2, Manoj Shah, 17, Richard McManus, 13, Wokephoto17, 21; Pexels/Miguel Cuenca, cover; Unsplash/David Valentine, 1, Lesly Derksen, 7, Luca Ambrosi, 18, Mark Flanagan, 16, Pat Whelen, 23, Sies Kranen, 5, Simone Millward, 9; Wikimedia Commons/Arifinal0109, 14, Bernard DUPONT, 10, Colin Knowles, 20, Tim Laman, 6

Cataloging-in-Publication data is available from
the Library of Congress.
Library Binding ISBN: 9798895810576
Paperback ISBN: 9798896800101
eBook ISBN: 9798895811832
LCCN: 2025011190

Printed in China

Table of Contents

Orangutans are members of the great ape family. Great apes have big brains. They have thumbs that are used to grasp things. Orangutans once lived across southeast Asia. Today, they are only found in Sumatra and Borneo.

Gorillas, chimpanzees, and people are part of the great ape family.

Borneo and Sumatra are large islands. They are the third- and sixth-largest in the world.

There are three **species** of orangutans. They are Bornean, Sumatran, and Tapanuli. The Tapanuli were not discovered until 2017. There are fewer than 800 left in the wild. But all three species are almost **extinct**.

species a group of animals with similar characteristics

extinct no longer living

Male orangutans are much larger than females. Females weigh between 80 and 120 pounds (36.3 and 54.4 kilograms). Males can weigh up to 220 pounds (99.8 kg). Males have broader chests and longer hair.

Orangutans in zoos are much bigger than those in the wild. They are fed high-quality food every day.

Orangutans spend a lot of time in trees. They swing, climb, and walk from branch to branch. They will also walk on the ground if they have to. Orangutans walk on their hind legs or on all fours.

Long red or orange fur helps orangutans blend into the treetops.

Orangutans spend around 60 percent of their day looking for food.

Orangutans are **omnivores**. They eat more than 2,000 different fruits and plant species. They also eat insects and small animals, such as lizards or birds. Mushrooms, eggs, and honey are other favorite meals.

omnivore an animal that eats both plants and animals

Orangutans usually live alone. They may spend time together when there is plenty of food. Males make booming noises called long calls. These calls attract females. They also tell other males to stay away.

A long call can be heard from almost a mile (1.6 kilometers) away.

Mating pairs are only together for a few days. One or two babies are born seven or eight months later. Orangutan babies stay with their mothers until they are eight years old. They come back to visit into their teens.

Baby orangutans cling to their mothers' bodies for the first two years of their lives.

Orangutans can live to around age 50.

Orangutans are not mature until they are around 12. Males continue growing for another 5 to 10 years. They may grow longer fur, beards, larger throat sacs, and face pads called **flanges**. Females are more attracted to flanged males.

flange a flat surface that sticks out

Orangutans can make and use tools. They dig with sticks and branches. Large leaves are used for shelter or clothing. Captive orangutans have been taught how to use stone tools. That's a smart ape!

Mother orangutans teach their offspring how to find food and survive.

An Orangutan Tale

The name

"orangutan" comes from a Dayak word that means "people of the forest." The Dayaks are the native people of Borneo. One of their tales says that God created orangutans first. People were made on the second day. Orangutans could talk but chose not to. They did not want to become slaves to humans. To avoid being caught, they climbed into the trees and stayed there.

Read More

Dell, Pamela. *Orangutan*. Mankato, Minn.: Creative Education/Creative Paperbacks, 2026.

Watt, E. Melanie. *Orangutan*. New York: Lightbox Learning Inc., 2025.

Websites

National Geographic Kids: Orangutan
https://kids.nationalgeographic.com/animals/mammals/facts/orangutan
Learn fun facts about orangutans.

Orangutan Conservancy
https://kids.orangutan.com/
An introduction to orangutans.

Index